GEORGE WASHINGTON CARVER

He was born in the 1860's on a horse farm in Diamond Grove, Missouri. His parents were George and Mary. His master was Moses—Moses Carver. Yes, George Carver was born a slave; nevertheless, he would become one of the most respected men in America. One day this farm on which he was born would be declared a national monument.

George Washington
CARVER

Written by Robert Hogrogian
Illustrated by Joe C. DePietro

JANUARY PRODUCTIONS

Library of Congress Catalog Card No.: 80-81929

ISBN: 0-934898-58-8 (library edition)
ISBN: 0-934898-08-1 (paperback)

When George was only a baby, a terrible thing happened. It happened one night when the Carvers were sleeping. Suddenly, the stillness of the night was broken. They heard the voice of a woman crying out.

"Run, James, run!" she screamed.

Then a man's voice shouted, "Take the woman! Take the brat. The other one got away. Hurry up before Old Man Carver comes with his gun!"

"My baby! My baby!" cried the woman. "Please don't hurt my baby!"

Then there was silence.

George's brother James had escaped. George and his mother were stolen by the night raiders. It was a common occurrence. They could get good money for the woman. She was only 19.

Mrs. Carver was heartbroken. She loved Mary as though she were one of her family. "You have to get them back, Moses," she begged. "You will get them back, won't you?"

"I don't know, Sue," he answered. "They must be long gone by now. I'll see what I can do."

Moses Carver asked around. He tried to find someone who knew what had become of Mary and her baby. Finally, he met a man named Bentley. Bentley claimed to know their whereabouts.

"You get them back for me," Moses said to him, "and I'll give you one of my best horses. I'll give you forty acres of land, too."

Bentley agreed. He and his sidekicks set out to find them.

Bentley couldn't find Mary. The outlaws had already sold her. They hadn't bothered with George. He was too small. They just left him. He was soaking wet and shivering from the cold when Bentley found him.

Bentley brought the child to Moses Carver. "You keep your land," he said. "I'll just take the horse."

In 1865 The Civil War was over. There were no longer any slaves. George and his brother James stayed with the Carvers anyway. The Carvers were the only family they knew.

For George and James—like everyone else on the farm—work always came first. George was a sickly child, but work had to be done, sick or not. James was much stronger and healthier. He did most of the heavy work. Mr. Carver was strict with the boys. Still, he treated them much as he would have treated his own sons.

The Carvers could not help but see the wonderful way George had with plants. In his spare time he walked in the woods. He stared up at the majestic trees in awe. The plants and seedlings were his friends. He talked to them. He sang to them. It seemed as though they loved the touch of his little hands.

The first thought of the boy's schooling came when George was about ten. George had gone with Mr. Carver to visit Herman Jaegar. What impressed George most was the special glass house that Mr. Jaegar had. It was a wonderful place where things grew the whole year round.

George explored the greenhouse. Here he saw plants more beautiful than he had imagined. Here he watched Mr. Jaegar graft slips of imported vines onto the native vines. The result was the sweetest grapes young George had ever tasted.

There was an immediate understanding between the man and the boy. They both loved growing things more than anything else. When it was time to leave, Mr. Jaegar presented him with a book.

"But, sir," said George, "I can read very little."

"Then you must go to school. There's one right around here," Mr. Jaegar explained.

The school he referred to was in Neosho. It was built by the Freedmen's Bureau. This bureau had been set up by Congress. Its main purpose was to help former slaves. One of its goals was to build schools for Black children.

School! George's heart leaped within him. To be able to read about plants and growing things was the most wonderful thing he could imagine. He made up his mind that this was the right thing to do. The Carvers agreed. They would not stand in his way.

George put on his Sabbath suit. He wrapped his belongings in a big bandanna handkerchief. He said good-bye to the three people he loved most. It was hard to leave James and the Carvers. At the age of 12 George Carver was on his own.

George's main problem was money. He went from place to place looking for odd jobs. He would have to earn enough to pay for room and board and books while at school.

George saw a fine, beautiful house on a hill. He straightened his back. Then he marched up and knocked on the door. He got up the courage to speak.

"Sir," he said, "I'd like to tend to your gardening. I'm awfully good at it. I can tend your fires in the mornings, too."

"You look a mite puny for such work," the man replied.

"I'm stronger than I look. You'll see. You won't be sorry."

"All right, we'll try it out. I'll give you 50 cents a week."

Jobs weren't always so easy to find. George's appearance was not reassuring. To those who didn't know him, there seemed to be a lack of strength and endurance. There was a certain strangeness about him.

One of the best things to happen to George was meeting a Black woman named Mariah Watkins. Her house was near the school. George had sat down to rest. Mariah saw him sitting there. She was very kind. She and her husband took him in. George was glad. He was tired of sleeping in barns.

George continued to work at any job he could find. In spite of his appearance, he was a good worker. He gave proof of his worth with every job—especially in the garden. People no longer turned him away. He was very much in demand.

In the meantime George continued to go to school. The teacher, Stephen Frost, held classes in a shabby one-room cabin. Seventy-five children of all ages were crowded together. They sat on the high, hard benches of the tiny room. George was extremely bright. He quickly mastered all the teacher could teach.

It was Aunt Mariah—as he came to call her—who first mentioned moving on. "It's time for you to go on to higher schools, George," she said. "You've learned all Mr. Frost knows to teach you. As much as I'll miss you, I think it's for the best."

George agreed. He had heard of a family moving from Neosho, Missouri, to Fort Scott, Kansas. He asked them to take him along. There was a high school there. Besides, George was still sickly. The climate there would be better for him.

George was about 16 when he arrived at Fort Scott. Again he searched for jobs. He managed to find a job as a cook. He did laundry. Then he went to school. When his money ran out, he again went to work. Each time he worked long enough to pay for his books.

It was during these wandering years that George Carver added the "W" to his name. He was living in Minneapolis, Kansas, at the time. There was another George Carver living in the same town. Letters written to George were being sent to this other man. George added the "W" to stop the confusion. People asked him what the letter stood for.

"Washington," he replied proudly. "I've always admired the man who would not tell a lie."

From that time on he was known as George Washington Carver.

George worked and studied hard. Blessed with a keen mind, he left his classmates far behind. Finally, a man in his early twenties, he was graduated from high school. He left Minneapolis, Kansas, and headed back to Diamond Grove, Missouri.

George was anxious to get home. He was saddened to learn that his brother James had died of small pox. He was happy, however, to see his old friends, the Carvers.

Sue and Moses Carver were delighted at George's advancement. "I'm right proud of you, George," said Moses Carver. "I guess you were worth the ransom I paid for you—even if it was a prize winning horse—but what are your plans now, George?"

What were his plans? George had given it much thought.

"Well," he said "you know how I love plants. But what I love most of all is painting them. I'd like to go to college to take some courses in art."

When George was 25, he was accepted at Highland University. He used all his money to buy a typewriter and other supplies he would need. George was ecstatic.

His joy soon turned to disappointment. When he arrived at Highland, the administrators found out that he was a Negro. He was turned away. George was hurt, but he kept that hurt inside. He wouldn't let their prejudice get the best of him.

A couple of years later George headed for Iowa. He worked as a cook in a hotel. He opened laundries. He worked as hard as he could. His goal was to enter Simpson College at Indianola. George had heard about the art courses there.

In 1890 George was accepted at Simpson. Again there was a problem. The people in charge of curriculum told him that Blacks weren't allowed to enroll in art courses. They felt it was more in their interest to learn subjects that would help them earn a living.

"Why should you waste your time studying art?" they asked him. "Surely you want to earn a living!"

George didn't give up. His persistence paid off. The art director agreed to let him try the art course for two weeks. She and the other administrators would watch him. At the end of that time he would have to accept their decision.

For two weeks George showed them what he could do. At the end they had to give their consent. He had shown a degree of excellence they couldn't deny.

George was well-liked at Simpson. It didn't take long for everyone to recognize his superior qualities. Something bothered him, however. As much as he loved to paint, he thought of giving it up. He didn't care that painting wouldn't earn money for himself. He did care that it wouldn't do anything to help others of his race. George decided to study agriculture instead.

The teachers at Simpson gave George wonderful recommendations. He had no trouble getting into the Iowa State College of Agriculture at Ames. He continued to be an exceptional student. In 1894 he was even elected poet laureate of his graduating class—an honor saved for the very best students.

George decided to go on for his master's degree. He became the first black graduate student at Ames. He also became their first black faculty member. George had been appointed Assistant Station Botanist of the college.

It was during this period that George's fame began to spread. He had become an expert at cross-breeding and grafting of plants. He had also become known for his work in mycology, the study of fungi. Before long, people from all over were asking his advice about plant diseases.

In 1896 George Washington Carver received a letter from another great Black American—Booker T. Washington. Booker T. Washington had built the Tuskegee Institute in Alabama. He had wanted Blacks to have a place to go to learn a vocation. Washington wanted George to join his staff at Tuskegee.

It was not an easy decision. George's salary at Tuskegee would be only $1,500. He would earn much more than that at Ames. Those at Ames begged him to stay. George was a valuable addition to their staff.

George decided to go to Tuskegee. That was where he could best help his people. There was great poverty in the South. Most of the Blacks there depended upon agriculture. An expert in agricultural science was needed. George Washington Carver would be that expert.

George knew that the root of the problem in the South was the one-crop system. They depended too much upon cotton. His plan was to educate the people—both black and white. He would teach them about soil conservation. He would teach them about crop rotation. He would explain the dangers of a one-crop system. Then he would help them cultivate other native crops, like peanuts and sweet potatoes.

George set up an experiment station. Every morning at four he went into the woods. He gathered specimens for his work. His experiments were endless. Could the original plant of the potato be improved? What if he grafted it with another? Could the taste be made sweeter? And the peanut—what could be done with it?

His experiments with peanuts led to the discovery of shampoos, soaps and 19 new shades of dyes. His work with vegetable oil led to a cure for infantile paralysis. While experimenting with the sweet potato, he discovered a paste for shoe-blacking. These were just a few of the products he developed.

George could have profited from all these discoveries. He chose not to. George himself never accepted any money for advice he gave. Neither would he take out any patents on his products. He wanted everyone to benefit from his findings—not just a few. George even turned down a contract to earn over $100,000. The offer was made by Thomas Alva Edison. He wanted George to join his staff. George refused. The money didn't even tempt him. He stuck to his $1,500 a year salary at Tuskegee. That's where he was needed most.

In 1920 George Carver was asked by the United Peanut Association to appear before Congress. He was to speak to the Ways and Means Committee about the potential uses of the peanut. They were there to discuss a tariff on the plant.

"Are we to waste our time discussing a tariff on peanuts?" asked one congressman. "Who cares about peanuts? Their only use is as monkey food!"

George stood to address the committee. He was wearing his shabby suit with a flower in his lapel as he always did. As he walked forward he heard the gibes of the audience. He simply ignored the remarks.

"Who are you?" asked the chairperson.

"I've come as a representative of the United Peanut Growers Association," he explained. "I've had some experience at the Tuskegee Institute in Alabama. I can tell you things about the peanut that will surprise you. They'll make you stop thinking of it as the lowly peanut."

"I'll give you ten minutes," said the chairperson. "We've wasted enough time on this monkey food."

"Gentlemen, did you know that peanuts are one of the richest products of the soil?" George began.

He introduced them to milk, to instant coffee, to buttermilk and to Worcestershire sauce—all derived from peanuts. And the learned gentlemen listened. They sat in disbelief as he described the hundreds of other products derived from the peanut. They became so engrossed in what he said that they ignored the time limit.

"Did you conduct all the research work yourself?" a voice asked.

"I did, sir, with the help of those at the research laboratory. We also experimented with the sweet potato. We haven't found quite as many uses for that plant—only 107. Of course, we're still working on it."

George told them more about the sweet potato; he told them more about the peanut. His ten minutes turned into one hour and forty-five minutes. When he finished, everyone stood and applauded.

George toured the South. He talked to farmers. He lectured at colleges. Some groups were hostile at first. George usually won them over in a few minutes. He did a lot to create understanding among Blacks and Whites. He never refused to give advice to anyone who invited him to speak. His fame grew.

Many awards and honors were bestowed upon George. In 1928 he was made an honorary Doctor of Science at Simpson College. In 1935 he was appointed to the United States Department of Agriculture. He was to serve as Collaborator in the Mycology and Plant Disease Survey Bureau. He received the Roosevelt medal for distinguished service in the field of science in 1939. People from all over the world travelled to Tuskegee—just to talk to Dr. Carver.

George Washington Carver always put the welfare of others before his own. On January 5, 1943, George Washington Carver died. The entire world mourned the loss of a great scientist, a great educator and, above all, a great man.

Big Hollow Middle School
26051 W. Nippersink Rd.
Ingleside, IL 60041